EERO

# SAARINEN ON HIS WORK

*A selection of buildings dating from 1947 to 1964*

*with statements by the architect, edited by Aline B. Saarinen*

*New Haven and London: Yale University Press, 1962*

# Architects and Architecture

On the Scope and Purpose
of Architecture

I think of architecture as the total of man's man-made physical surroundings. The only thing I leave out is nature. You might say it is man-made nature. It is the total of everything we have around us, starting from the largest city plan, including the streets we drive on and its telephone poles and signs, down to the building and house we work and live in and does not end until we consider the chair we sit in and the ash tray we dump our pipe in. It is true that the architect practices on only a narrow segment of this wide keyboard, but that is just a matter of historical accident. The total scope is much wider than what he has staked his claim on. So, to the question, what is the scope of architecture? I would answer: It is man's total physical surroundings, outdoors and indoors.

Now, what is the purpose of architecture? Here again I would stake out the most ambitious claim. I think architecture is much more than its utilitarian meaning – to provide shelter for man's activities on earth. It is certainly that, but I believe it has a much more fundamental role to play for man, almost a religious one. Man is on earth for a very short time and he is not quite sure what his purpose is. Religion gives him his primary purpose. The permanence and beauty and meaningfulness of his surroundings give him confidence and a sense of continuity. So, to the question, what is the purpose of architecture, I would answer: To shelter and enhance man's life on earth and to fulfill his belief in the nobility of his existence. [Dickinson College, December 1, 1959]

On Architecture

We are in one of the great formative periods right now. It began about 1900 and it may last for the rest of the century. The ground rules and the general direction have been set, but there is still much to be done before the form of our time really emerges. During such a period we have to remain alert and flexible. New structural materials, new uses, a new spirit of our age. Yes, we are facing new frontiers. This is not a period of refinement. [Museum of Modern Art, March 11, 1952]

Esthetically, we have an urge to soar great distances with our new materials and to reach upward and outward. In a way, this is man's desire to conquer gravity. All the time one works, one concerns oneself with the fight against gravity. Everything tends to be too heavy and downward pressing unless one really works at it. [To a friend, June 3, 1953]

Our architecture is too humble. It should be prouder, more aggressive, much richer and larger than we see it today. I would like to do my part in expanding that richness. [*Time,* July 2, 1956]

I feel strongly that modern architecture is in danger of falling into a mold too quickly – too rigid a mold. What once was a great hope for a great new period of architecture has somehow become an automatic application of the same formula over and over again everywhere. I feel, therefore, a certain responsibility to examine problems with the specific enthusiasm of bringing out of the particular problem the particular solution.

It could well be thought that this shifting of the ground rules is a lack of conviction or a lack of direction on my part. Whether it is or not, of course, only time will tell. But my belief is sincerely that we must explore and expand the horizons of our architecture. In this sense, I align myself humbly with Le Corbusier and against Mies van der Rohe, although I admire his achievements immensely. [To German colleagues, July 22, 1958]

I am a child of my period. I am enthusiastic about the three common principles of modern architecture: function, structure, and being part of our time. The principle of respecting function is deeply imbedded in me as it is in others of this period. But, like others, I do not look to it to solve my architectural problems. Sometimes, however, the problem and the time are ripe for an entirely new functional approach to a problem (as in the new jet airport for Washington), and at such moments function may become the overwhelming principle in directing the formula of design.

The principle of structure has moved in a curious way over this century from being 'structural honesty' to 'expression of structure' and finally to 'structural expressionism.' Structural integrity is a potent and lasting principle and I would never want to get far away from it. To express structure, however, is not an end in itself. It is only when structure can contribute to the total and to the other principles that it is important.

The third common principle of modern architecture – the awareness of the thinking and technology of our time – is for me an ever-present challenge. I want always to search out the new possibilities in new materials of our time and to give them their proper place in architectural design.

Yes, I am dedicated to these three basic principles of modern architecture. But it seems to me they are not necessarily the only pillars one's work must rest on. The great architecture of the past did not rest on these alone. There are other principles equally or more important.

When I approach an architectural problem, I try to think out the real significance of the problem. What is its essence and how can the total structure capture that essence? How can the whole building convey emotionally the purpose and meaning of the building? Conveying significant meaning is part of the inspirational purpose of architecture and, therefore, for me, it is a fundamental principle of our art.

The conviction that a building cannot be placed on a site, but that a building grows from its site, is another principle in which I believe. I see architecture not as the building alone, but the building in relation to its surroundings, whether nature or man-made surroundings. I believe very strongly that the single building must be carefully related to the whole in the outdoor space it creates. In its mass and scale and material it must become an enhancing element in the total environment. Now this does not mean that the building has to succumb to the total. Any architecture must hold its head high. But a way must be found for uniting the whole, because the total environment is more important than the single building.

The external form of my work varies greatly. But inside the solution of every

I see architecture not as the building alone,
but the building in relation to its surroundings, whether nature or man-made surroundings [Saarinen's music tent,
Aspen, Colorado, 1952]

problem there are underlying principles that hold it together and join each building I have done to every other one. In fact, if it didn't sound too pompous, I would say that the common denominator of my work is the constant philosophy – the constant respect for the principles in which I believe. [Dickinson College, December 1, 1959]

On Architecture of the Past

**B**ecause we feel confident in our period, we can look at the past and derive inspiration instead of falling into imitation. [To A.I.A., June 16, 1954]

Naturally, I do not believe in eclecticism or imitation, but I think that it is very important every now and then to look carefully at the architecture of other times so that we can test the degree of fulfillment of our architecture against the degree of fulfillment of theirs. It is a terribly good way to knock the pins out from under our smugness. [To A.I.A., April 4, 1957]

On Federal Architecture

**I** have no objection to the classic spirit. For government buildings, such a spirit should prevail. But not the *style* or the *dilution* of the style. That is where the mistake is made. [To a student, April 18, 1958]

On the Practice of Architecture

**Y**ou young architects will find the twin qualities necessary for an architect are humility and 'crust.' Humility for the problem and the realities; 'crust' for solving the problem and sticking with the essentials of the solution. [I.I.T., April 30, 1956]

I think sometimes architecture is like a marvelous three-dimensional chess game. Every move or decision affects every other move and decision. You have to keep thinking about and juggling all the parts at the same time. In general, if I had to say how we work, I guess it would be that we start by considering very carefully the problem of the site, the problem of the program, and the problem of the spirit of the particular job. We really try to look into these things very thoroughly. They all go on at the same time. Then we start gradually trying to put the answers to these problems together and then, with them, we start putting in the structural system.

If everything goes well and everything is really performing within one idea and the structural system is the right one, with the right materials and methods and so on, *it* becomes the thing which locks everything together. When that happens, it is a marvelous feeling. The structural system then seems to reinforce an inevitable solution to the site problem, and, at the same time, an inevitable solution to the functional problems and, at the same time, an inevitable solution to the spirit. All these things get locked together into one thing. [To a student, August 20, 1960]

Intuition plays a large part in architecture, because we don't have an IBM machine big enough to take all the factors into consideration. So, you depend on intuition. But, boy! wherever you can apply straight thinking or IBM machine methods or things like that, you absolutely have to do it. [*Horizon* interview, June 19, 1959]

The stumbling block in this easy way to approval and success is my stubborn interpretation of the integrity of an architect. I realize fully well that our preliminary design was not liked and has been criticized. My solution is to redesign, which I am now in the process of doing. I have never gone into a political alliance in architecture and I never will.

I would like to get philosophical about all this and relate it to love: architecture is my great love and as such I propose to practice it. If I ever have to practice it with middlemen involved, it would cease to become my enthusiasm. [To a suggestion that he form an association in name only with a native architect in order to get a foreign design approved, March 8, 1961]

What you newspaper and magazine writers, who work in rabbit time, don't understand is that the practice of architecture has to be measured in elephant time. [To a journalist, February 14, 1953]

I appreciate your recognition that I have chosen a hard life. It is lots of fun and I wouldn't want it to be any different, but actually it *is* hard. Sometimes a design comes easily and the result turns out well, but sometimes the design doesn't 'come' and it becomes harder and harder and one loses one's perspective. But one has to drive oneself as well as everyone else to make it come out as well as possible.

Then one has to nurse these babies through an endless number of months while clients and clients' representatives try to butcher them. This is a tiresome process with fight after fight and long-drawn-out meeting after meeting. Then, after all that is over, one has to take on the intelligentsia shooting at one from the hip. [To a friend, March 27, 1961]

One of the problems I have been facing lately more than ever is the reshuffling of client executives. Each time there is a change of executives on a job, the whole design always hangs in the balance. To face these problems, to fight these post-design wars, to have to defend everything from the color of tile on toilet walls to door handles takes almost more time than the original design. I have good and able partners and associates, but most of the time these fights and strategies cannot be delegated.

Exactly how long a design will take is a most unpredictable thing. At the moment, I am working on two. One may look simple, but it has been an enormous struggle. In spite of all our efforts, we may not have found a very good solution. The other has come together more easily and simply than I ever imagined a design could and it looks like one of our very best buildings and is almost on schedule. I guess what all this boils down to is that I should never give anybody any schedules. One cannot do what I am trying to do within schedules. [To a client, April 18, 1961]

On the Individual in Architecture

It is on the individual, his sensitivities and understanding, that our whole success or failure rests. He must recognize that this is a new kind of civilization in which the artist will be used in a new and different way. The neat categories of bygone days do not hold true any longer. His job requires a curious combination of intuition and 'crust.' He must be sensitive and adaptable to trends and needs; he must be part of and understand our civilization. At the same time, he is not just a mirror; he is also a co-creator and must have the strength and urge to produce form, not compromise. [*Seventy-Five,* Yale publication, 1953]

Today, when so much stress is laid on the common denominator, on teamwork, on a vernacular, on the impersonal, we tend to forget the importance of the individual. Such thinking does us serious harm. It sanctions the practice of making the little boy in the back room a designer and making design a mere commodity to be sold by the front sales office.

Great architecture is both universal and individual. The universality is achieved because the architecture is a true expression of its time. The individuality comes through – as at Illinois Institute of Technology – as a result of a special quality. It is a quality that is perhaps the least understood of all. It is a quality that cannot be taught. This quality is the philosophy and thinking behind architecture: it is the expression of one man's unique combination of faith and honesty and devotion and beliefs in architecture, in short, his moral integrity.

Great architecture is always informed by one man's thinking. We can borrow and build on someone else's philosophy, but we must evolve our own. The important lesson is the absolute necessity of having a philosophy, or, as Mies calls it, 'a spiritual orientation.' [I.I.T., April 30, 1956]

Unlike painting and sculpture, where the individual works entirely alone, architecture involves many people. It is true that it all has to be siphoned through one mind, but there is always teamwork. [Dickinson College, 1959]

On Drawing

To me the drawn language is a very revealing language: one can see in a few lines whether a man is really an architect. [To a student, May 23, 1961]

On Expression and Unity

We need an expanded vocabulary because modern architecture is now mature enough to think about bigger problems of expression.

Perhaps expression does not seem too much of a problem for the ordinary buildings that are really just part of what might be called a 'building-scape,' a sort of background scenery. But I think we could argue that even these should have an expression: the modest one of being what they are. Expression is crucial in the special building. [R.I.B.A., June 12, 1957]

The character or expression of any building can only be achieved if it is itself a total expression. Like any work of art, it must be dominated by a strong, simple concept. All of its parts must be an active part of one dominant attitude. This is true whether the elements and decisions are big, early ones, like plan and structural system, or later ones, like interior color and doorknobs. This challenge of making a building a total expression seems to me the highest and most difficult one. But it is the one that I think must concern all of us most. [R.I.B.A., June 12, 1957]

Architecture must make a strong emotional impact on man. I have come to the conviction that once one embarks on a concept for a building, this concept has to be exaggerated and overstated and repeated in every part of its interior, so that wherever you are, inside or outside, the building sings with the same message. [Dickinson College, December 1, 1959]

In any kind of design, one has to go fearlessly ahead to the most rational, most clear, and most intense consequence. [Munich, October 24, 1960]

On Relationships in Design

Every object, small or large, has a relationship to its neighbors. Perhaps the most important thing I learned from my father was that in any design problem one should seek the solution in terms of the next largest thing. If the problem is an ashtray, then the way it relates to a table will influence its design. If the problem is a chair, then its solution must be found in the way it relates to the room cube. If it is a building, the townscape will affect the solution. [s.i.d., June 19, 1958]

On Plastic Form in Architecture

We should proceed into the field of plastic form with caution. Plastic form uncontrolled by structure rings a hollow note. [a.i.a., June 16, 1954]

Technology has made plastic form easily possible for us. But it is the esthetic reasons which are the driving forces behind its use.

What interests me is when and where to use these structural plastic shapes. Probing ever more deeply into different possibilities one finds many different shapes are equally logical – some ugly, some exciting, some earthbound, some soaring. The choices really become sculptor's choices. But we must beware of going too far. Architectural form cannot become all sculpture. Plastic form for its own sake, even when very virile, does not seem to come off. [r.i.b.a., June 12, 1957]

On Interior Design

The ideal interior is one that grows together with and out of the total concept of a building. In a sense, it grows the way chromosomes multiply out of the original sperm and the thinking of the total concept is carried down to the smallest detail. This organic unity is the ideal. It is the possibility when the problem involves a special, total building, such as an airport, a church, or a custom-built house.

Usually the problem of interior design is limited. It begins within the existing framework of an office, apartment, or ready-made house.

The shells of these living and working units have to answer the needs of hundreds of thousands of people. They have become completely anonymous shells. And thank God this is so! It is when they stray from strict impersonality – and try to anticipate some personal idiosyncrasy by mass-producing some kind of fancy door-moulding or mantelpiece – that these living and working shells for a mass market fail both practically and esthetically.

Likewise, furniture has moved from the handicraft era into a mass-production era and so, to a greater or lesser degree, have other items of the interior. The result is that the major equipment or furnishings of the interior have an impersonal character. As with the architectural shells, it is essential, in fact, that a mass-produced item must have this impersonal character. It must not be romantic, in the sense of answering a special problem or smacking of the artist's personality. It must be classic, in the sense of responding to an often-recurring need, both practical and visual, in many different situations.

Most people want to create for themselves not only an orderly twentieth-century environment but they want also to make an environment which is an expression of their personal identities.

I would like to state very strongly that I do not see any conflict between these desires – on the one hand, for a truly twentieth-century environment which accepts in full the impersonality of both setting and furnishings and, on the other, the desire for a truly personal expression in the interior. I believe there can be a very beautiful result when the interior reflects both desires without any compromise of either.

The virtually mass-produced walls, spaces, and furniture must never lose their impersonal character: they are to the interior as structure is to architecture.

But playing against them are what we can call the ornamental or non-structural elements. These are such objects as paintings and sculptures, flowers, vases, heirlooms, books, legitimately handicraft objects from travel or exotic parts of the world or the past, and so on. They may be small in volume and small in number, but they assume significance and strength in the impersonal, noncommittal setting. They stand out like oases in the desert. They express the personality and establish the identity of the owners.

Things go wrong when the differentiation is not clearly stated. The failures usually come from an overanxiousness to create the personal at the expense of the impersonal. This is a watering down of principles. It leads inevitably to compromise and to confusion.

Compromise usually comes from a fear of being pure. A hankering for the past leads to a compromise with the present. Confusion comes from trying to amalgamate several conflicting ideas in one room. A room is like a piece of art: it is just one idea. This idea can have many variations on the same theme, but it cannot have many themes. Compromise and confusion are qualities alien to good interiors, just as they are alien to good architecture and good people. [Munich, October 24, 1960]

When an interior is really successful, the compensations for all the effort are tremendous. The clarity and serenity of a good interior give an absolutely marvelous feeling of strength with which to face our complicated and confused world. The fact that one has achieved this atmosphere with the form-world and technology of one's own era gives further satisfaction. And finally the psychological satisfaction of having expressed an identity is deeply rewarding. Especially in a world of standardization of people as well as things, this coherent, clear expression of one's own individuality is a necessary goal. [Munich, October 24, 1960]

On Campus
Planning

I am very interested in campus planning. Universities are to our time what the monasteries were to the Middle Ages. They are oases in our desert-like civilization. They also have about the only beautiful pedestrian spaces that are left to us. And it may turn out that they have our only permanent architecture. On new campuses there is the opportunity of achieving total, beautiful twentieth-century environments that have unity and order. On existing campuses, there is the challenge of building proud buildings of our own time that are in harmony with the outdoor space and with the existing buildings of other times. [To a friend, March 24, 1953]

An architect must be conscientiously responsible toward the master plan and he must be conscientiously responsible toward all the buildings around. There is always a way – not necessarily within the current enthusiasms – or a way must be invented so that the old which is good does not become obsolete because of its new neighbor. [*Architectural Record,* November, 1960]

I think there is a great advantage if a group of buildings can all be done under the responsibility of one architect. Different areas of a campus can have different characters. But we could stand more unity within each area. I am beginning to long for monotony. [To a friend, May 31, 1960]

On Urban Planning and Design

The total environment is the real problem and, in a sense, the new frontier of architecture. [To a Polish architect, October 1, 1959]

The challenge for architects today is to find a larger discipline so that we can make of our cities homogeneous things instead of the Klondike-type chaos which they are today. [To students, June 1, 1960]

The urban redevelopment plans now in progress from coast to coast sometimes have fine answers to a limited problem. But they all have one very important lack in common: they lack the vision and conviction of a total visual concept. They have not found for our time what Baron Haussmann found for the Paris of his time: a complete visual order.

Today we have a certain manner of using high towers and low buildings in our urban redevelopment plans. (It is really based on Le Corbusier's concept of how a city should look, but it has not been very well developed.) The core of the problem of placing high towers in vast reclaimed areas is the vistas between these towers. The strategic question is our ability to enclose or to define space with these independent building blocks.

Some twenty years ago there was great enthusiasm for the so-called 'open plan' in our houses—a plan where one space flowed into the next. This was hailed as a new and dynamic space concept. Much was written about it, but very little wonderful or great came out of it.

Today, many of us have come back to much more 'closed' plans, where rooms are really rooms with four walls. I suspect that in the re-thinking of the urban picture we might be coming to a similar conclusion: we may want to place our buildings in such a manner that we can achieve an orderly and legible space between them. [Benjamin Franklin Lecture, December 8, 1960]

No generation has talked so much about 'outdoor space' as ours and none has done so little about it. [*Architectural Record,* November, 1960]

The subject of urban planning and form interests me more and more as the crucial problem. [To a colleague, March 6, 1961]

On Frank Lloyd Wright

I agree that non-critical estimates of Frank Lloyd Wright are rather meaningless now. I would go further and say that critical estimates of Wright are also meaningless now. Sometime Frank Lloyd Wright will be re-evaluated—and his great concept of architecture where everything is all one organism, all one thing, will be appreciated. [To a friend, May 18, 1959]

On Himself I was a very lucky little boy. We, as a family, lived in Finland until I was twelve years old. My father had his architectural studio right in the house. The whole family would sit at one end of the studio. As a child, I would always draw and I happened to be good at it. Therefore, I got more attention from drawing than anything else. That made me draw more and more. Later, Maróti, a Hungarian sculptor who was a friend of my parents, took me in hand and made me really work at it. He made me draw from nature and study anatomy and he would make me do things over and over. I was only praised if what I did was good, not the way children are praised today for anything they do. [*New York Times* interview, January 29, 1953]

Except for a rather brief excursion into sculpture, it never occurred to me to do anything but to follow in my father's footsteps and become an architect. As his partner, I often contributed technical solutions and plans, but only within the concept he created. A better name for architect is form-giver and until his death in 1950, when I started to create my own form, I worked within the form of my father. [*New York Times*, April 26, 1953]

My father, Eliel Saarinen, was a fine architect and a leader in his generation. He has been given his own deserved recognition. I shall be grateful if my efforts are as successful. If they are, I would prefer to be recognized for my own success. [To proposal for a joint book, February 19, 1959]

I feel most humble and most appreciative of all the very nice, very complimentary things you said in your letter. I must admit that the statement my ego liked the most was 'methodical but not cautious architect.' That I liked especially. [To German colleagues, July 22, 1958]

In the end, you can only create and make decisions according to your own integrity. But it is true that I would also like the respect of architects I respect. [*New York Times* interview, January 29, 1953]

The only architecture which interests me is architecture as a fine art. That is what I want to pursue. I hope that some of my buildings will have lasting truths. I admit frankly I would like a place in architectural history. Whether I do or not and how big a niche depends, in the end, on native talent and one cannot ask for more than one has. But one has to work as hard as one can. [To a friend, October, 1952]

I think I now have a really good scheme for CBS. The design is the simplest conceivable rectangular free-standing sheer tower. The verticality of the tower is emphasized by the relief made by the triangular piers between the windows. These start at the pavement and soar up 491 feet. Its beauty will be, I believe, that it will be the simplest skyscraper statement in New York. [To the client, March 31, 1961]

From the beginning, I imagined CBS as a dark building. A dark building seemed more quiet and dignified and appropriate to this site. We learned from our Oslo embassy that a dark building looks well in a city.

It should also look permanent. I think too much modern architecture is flimsy-looking. One of the things I learned from my father is that a building should weather well. The CBS building should be a masonry building: concrete, clad in granite.

Now, as to the nature of the design. I wanted a building that would be a soaring thing. I think Louis Sullivan was right to want the skyscraper to be a soaring thing. I wanted a building that would stand firmly on the ground and would grow straight up. Your eyes should be led up to comprehend a building as a whole thing.

In the structure that we developed, we made a rectangular doughnut. We put a ring of concrete columns around the perimeter and a concrete core containing services and vertical transportation in the center. It permitted clear office space. We devised a plan to eliminate wasteful public corridors. We made efficient use of the mechanical system by putting one mechanical floor at the bottom and another at the top with office floors between them.

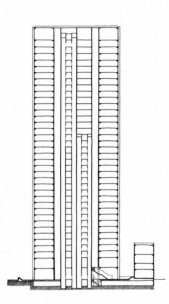

We arrived at the triangular piers after much study of other shapes. This shape emphasized verticality most strongly. It best combined mechanical and structural requirements. It was a simple shape to be clad in granite. It kept the glass area to a reasonable minimum. The triangular piers would make a changing relief as you moved around. You would see glass and granite; then solid granite with reflecting surfaces. We had learned the way a changing relief gives life to a façade.

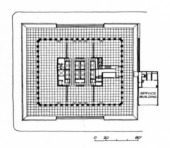

We tried to place the building on the site so that we could have a plaza and still not destroy the street line. A tower should not be tied in with lower street buildings. It should stand alone with air and light around it. A plaza is a very necessary thing in a city. It lets people sit in the sun and look at the sky. A plaza allows a building to be seen. Our buildings should be seen, because they are monuments of our time. But a plaza can be a dangerous thing. We have to remember the street line and we have to remember the space between is as important as the towers. These arrangements should be orderly and beautiful so the streets do not look like torn things and the towers like isolated teeth sticking up from a gaping mouth.

I am excited about the CBS building. I think that everything—siting, planning, structural, mechanical systems, spirit – has been brought to its logical conclusion. They are clearly expressed and locked into one thing. When you look at this building, you will know exactly what is going on. It is a very direct and simple structure. It does just what it has to do. But because it does it so simply and strongly, I think it may do something more – express the spirit of a building which by its nature must thrust upwards. I believe the spirit of a building should be expressed, not hidden behind a neutral curtain of glass. Buildings should have 'guts' and direction and make statements. Neutral buildings do not stimulate man's imagination or give man confidence or make him feel proud and I believe architecture should do these things. [*passim*, January to August 1961]

I n 1948, we won the national competition for a new national park in St. Louis, symbolizing and commemorating the westward expansion of America. The major concern here was to create a monument which would have lasting significance and would be a landmark of our time. An absolutely simple shape – such as the Egyptian pyramids or obelisks – seemed to be the basis of the great memorials that have kept their significance and dignity across time. Neither an obelisk nor a rectangular box nor a dome seemed right on this site or for this purpose. But here, at the edge of the Mississippi River, a great arch *did* seem right.

But what kind of an arch? We believed that to stand the test of time the arch had to be the purest expression of the forces within. This arch is not a true parabola, as is often stated. Instead it is a catenary curve – the curve of a hanging chain – a curve in which the forces of thrust are continuously kept within the center of the legs of the arch. The mathematical precision seemed to enhance the timelessness of the form, but at the same time its dynamic quality seemed to link it to our own time. The arch, as redesigned, is 630 feet high with a span of 630 feet. Fifty-six feet at the triangular bases, it tapers to eighteen feet at the apex. It seems now really to be an upward-thrusting form, not an earthbound one.

Having arrived at a shape that seemed to have permanence and to belong to our time, what material would also fulfill these two qualities? Stainless steel seemed the inevitable answer—and so we decided on stainless steel with a concrete core.

All these things seemed to come together to make a right monument for this place and for our time. The arch could be a triumphal arch for our age as the triumphal arches of classical antiquity were for theirs. Lofty, dynamic, of permanent significance, the arch could be a proper visual center and focus for the park and, as 'The Gateway to the West,' it could symbolize the spirit of the whole Memorial.

We believed that what downtown St. Louis most needed was a tree-covered park. We wanted to have the most nature possible toward the city.

The arch was placed near the Mississippi River, where it would have most significance. Here it could make a strong axial relation with the handsome, historic Old Courthouse which it frames. Here, from its summit, the public could confront the magnificent river. The arch would draw people to the superb view and picturesque activity at the river's edge. The museum, the restaurant, the historic riverboats were all projected on the levee. The river would be drawn into the total composition.

The arch will be on a raised plaza of about twenty-five feet. This base not only gives the arch more dominance over the tall buildings of the city, but it seemed essential as an approach to a vertical monument. On the levee side, this becomes a broad, monumental stairway (a symbolic stairway as well as an actual one, for it symbolizes the movement of peoples through St. Louis, the gateway). The stairs of which we built a part in full-size mock-up, have treads of decreasing depth toward the top to dramatize the upward sweep of the approach to the arch.

The formal elements of the plaza and the axial, tree-lined mall leading to the Old Courthouse are contrasted with the romantic areas on each side of the axis – areas with pools, rock outcroppings, and winding paths. All the lines of the site plan, including the paths and the roads, and even the railroad tunnels, have been brought into the same family of curves to which the great arch itself belongs. More and more I believe that all parts of an architectural composition must be parts of the same form-world. [January, 1959]

The other side of the river—East St. Louis—must be brought into the whole composition. We must make this a great, green park. [August 19, 1961]

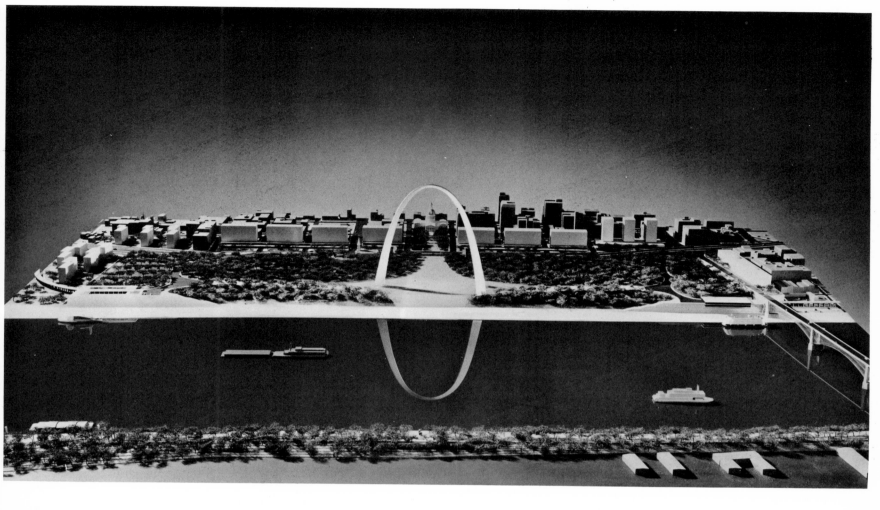

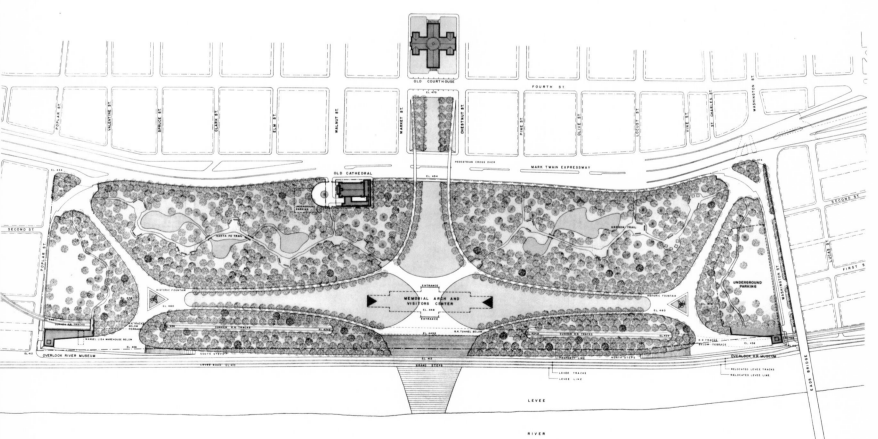

630 FEET

Our intention was threefold: to provide the best possible facilities for industrial research; to create a unified, beautiful, and human environment; and to find an appropriate architectural expression.

General Motors is a metal-working industry; it is a precision industry; it is a mass-production industry. All these things should, in a sense, be expressed in the architecture of its Technical Center.

Thus, the design is based on steel – the metal of the automobile. Like the automobile itself, the buildings are essentially put together, as on an assembly line, out of mass-produced units. And, down to the smallest detail, we tried to give the architecture the precise, well-made look which is a proud characteristic of industrial America. The architecture attempts to find its eloquence out of a consistent and logical development of its industrial character. It has been said that in these buildings I was very much influenced by Mies. But this architecture really carries forward the tradition of American factory buildings which had its roots in the Middle West in the early automobile factories of Albert Kahn.

Maximum flexibility was a prime requirement of the complicated program. It was achieved by applying the five-foot module not only to steel construction but also to laboratory, heating, ventilating, and fire-protection facilities as well as to laboratory furniture, storage units, wall partitions, and so on, all of which are keyed to it.

Now, as to the environment. The site occupies the central 320 acres of an approximately 900-acre area. The Center consists of five separate staff organizations – Research, Process Development, Engineering, Styling, and a Service Center as well as a central restaurant (in addition to cafeterias in the building groups). Each staff organization has its own constellation of buildings. There are twenty-five of these, including laboratory, office and shop buildings, and special use ones, like the two Dynamometer buildings.

Some sort of campus plan seemed right, but we were concerned with the problem of achieving an architectural unity with these horizontal buildings. The earlier scheme we made in 1945 had its great terrace and covered walk which unified the buildings into one great enterprise, but these had proved expensive and impractical. In the new scheme, developed when General Motors came back in 1948, we depended on simpler visual devices.

One of these is the twenty-two-acre pool. Not only does this form one dominant open space, but it also helps unity by providing a strong, hard architectural line and by strengthening all vertical dimensions of the buildings through their reflection.

Another unifying device is the surrounding forest, the green belt that should in time give the buildings the effect of being placed on the edge of a large glen. We gave very careful study to the placing and heights of the various buildings so they would form a controlled rhythm of high and low buildings, of glass walls and brick walls, of buildings seen between trees and buildings open to the square. Our basic design allowed variety within unity. The standardization of module throughout the project was arrived at for practical reasons, but we also hoped the constant use of this one dimension would have a unifying effect.

The use of color in an overall sense was devised, not only for its pleasing aspects, but also to help bind the project together. By an overall sense, I mean that color is not used in small ways on the exterior. The brilliant blues, reds, yellow, orange, black are on the great big end walls of buildings. Some of these are about forty feet

Photo
page
29

STYLING

DOME

Photo
page
33

ENGINEERING

Photo
page
31

FOUNTAIN

M O U N D   R O A D

RESTAURANT

MAIN GATE

Photo
pages
26 & 27

POOL

PROCESS
DEVELOPMENT

WATER TOWER

CALDER

WATER BALLET

SERVICE
CENTER

Photo
page
30

Staircase
photo
page
32

RESEARCH

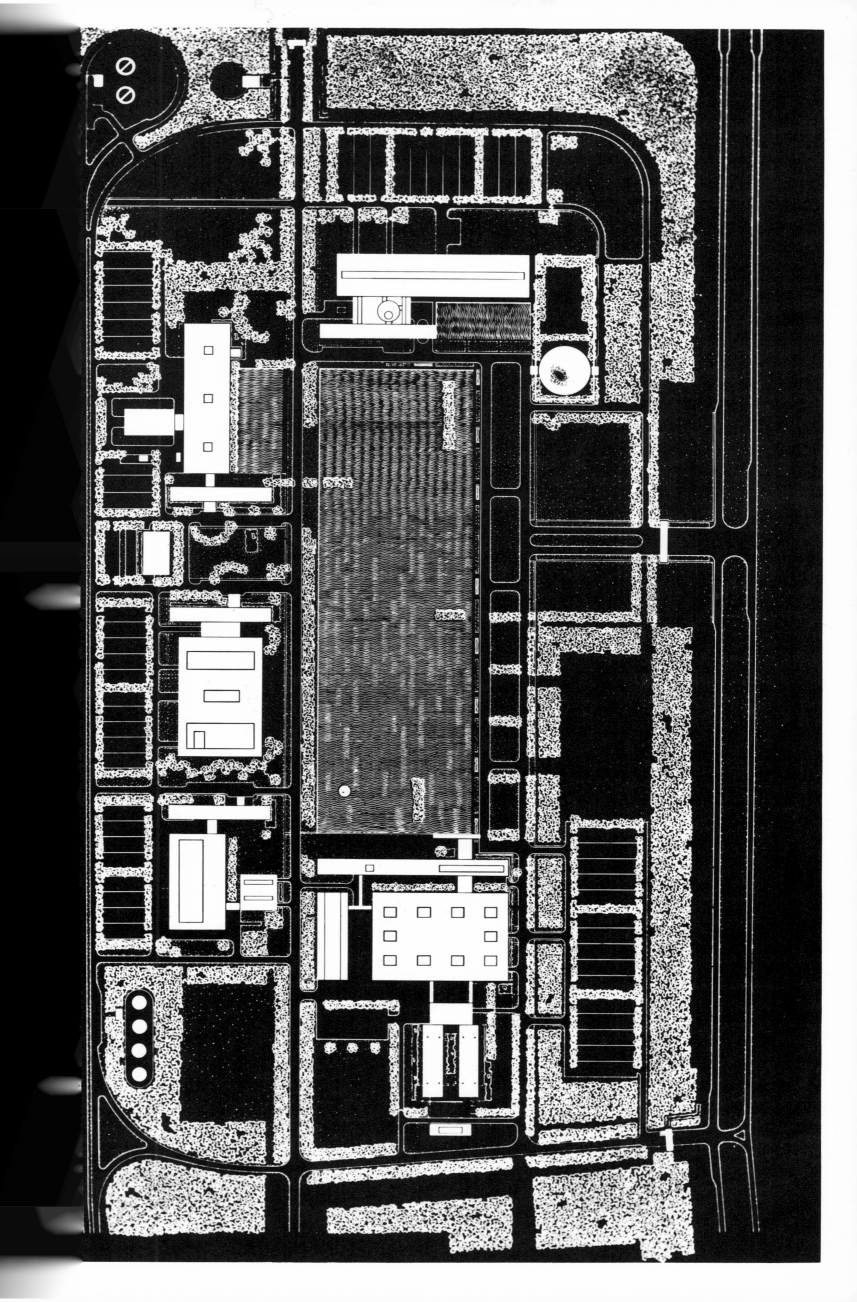

high and each is of one color, so they are rather like cards of color in space. Then all the glass and metal walls have certain standardized neutral colors.

In the earlier scheme, there was a tall administration building which gave the project a strong, vertical focal point. When that building was dropped from the program, we sought vertical focal points in other ways. Where the administration building would have been, we put the great fountain, a 115-foot-wide, fifty-foot-high wall of moving water. Then, instead of hiding the water tower, we designed it to be a proud 132-foot-high, stainless-steel-clad spherical shape and set it in the pool as a vertical accent in the whole composition. The water ballet with its playing jets, by Alexander Calder, is another visual accent near the Research building.

The Center was, of course, designed at automobile scale and the changing vistas were conceived to be seen as one drove around the project. However, opposite the water wall fountain, in front of the central restaurant, we deliberately created a little pedestrian-scale court.

Each of the staff organizations prides itself on its own individuality and its range of activities. Each wanted its own 'personality.' We tried to answer this desire architecturally in the main lobby of each of the five groups. In four of these, the visual climax to the lobby is the main staircase. These staircases are deliberately made into ornamental elements, like large-scale technological sculptures.

The public usually does not see the shop areas of the Center. We tried to keep the architectural character of the whole. They are generally wonderfully big open areas with long-span construction. We organized all the mechanical facilities with the structure so that we could avoid the usual slum-like appearance of factory buildings. We used color on the machines to make the areas visually agreeable and to unify them in the total environment. In the Dynamometer buildings, the free-standing exhaust pipes were designed to be strong elements in the composition.

One of the things we are proudest of is that, working together with General Motors, we developed many 'firsts' in the building industry. I think that this is part of the architect's responsibility.

We had previously used a baked enamel-finished panel on the Pharmacy Building at Drake University, which may well have been the very first instance of the now so familiar metal curtain wall. But General Motors represents the first significant installation of laminated panels and the first use anywhere of a uniquely thin porcelain-faced sandwich panel which is a complete prefabricated wall for both exterior and interior. For this project, we also developed the brilliantly colored glazed brick. The ceilings in the drafting rooms are the first developed completely luminous ceilings using special modular plastic pans. Perhaps the greatest gift to the building industry is the development of the neoprene gasket weather seal, which holds fixed glass and porcelain enamel metal panels to their aluminum frames. It is truly windproof and waterproof and is capable of allowing the glass or panels to be 'zipped out' whenever a building's use changes. All of these developments have become part of the building industry and a common part of the language of modern architecture. [*passim*, 1949–1957]

Every time I go to the Tech Center, I think what a great client General Motors was. The buildings are perfectly maintained. And they prove that in the long run good materials pay. The Engineering group is eight years old, but it looks as if it had been finished yesterday. [January 25, 1961]

As with all of our projects, in arriving at the concept we began with the basic considerations of the particular job: the program; the spirit or 'expression' of the program; the client; and the site with its surroundings, whether man-made or 'natural' nature.

Here, the site, in the middle of a crowded city campus, was surrounded by 'man-made' nature of buildings about six storeys high, buildings which were essentially boxes with holes pierced in them all around. The question was how to relate the auditorium to these buildings. Should we relate by blending with them or by making a contrast to them? We felt that a box-like structure in these surroundings, differing from the adjacent dormitories and apartment buildings only by the absence of windows, would be an undistinguished anticlimax. We believed that what was required was a contrasting silhouette, a form which started from the ground and went up, carrying the eye around its sweeping shape. Thus, a domed structure seemed right. There were other reasons, too, that influenced us toward a dome. There was the large dome of Welles Bosworth's central building at M.I.T. A dome is an economical way of covering an area with concrete. It is a shape which provides a pleasant atmosphere for an auditorium. And a thin-shell concrete structure seemed an appropriate form to express the spirit of this advanced school of technology.

One concept underlying auditorium design is to let the functional requirements – acoustics and sightlines – determine the form. But there is no one ideal acoustical shape. Though function has to be respected, it seemed equally justifiable to let the basic form come from structure. Thus, in developing the design of this building, we felt very strongly guided by Mies' principles of architecture – of a consistent structure and a forthright expression of that structure.

As there are many ways of doing equally functional things, we built dozens of models. As an auditorium requires a triangular shape, we tried spanning this one-room building with a dome supported at three points – the shape of one-eighth of an orange. At first it seemed strange, but gradually it became the loved one.

The auditorium floor, holding the seats, is essentially a reverse dome shape. The building was thus two shell shapes, like a clam. The acoustical requirements were well solved by the use of 'floating clouds.'

The exterior of the auditorium has generated a good deal of discussion, pro and con. I think some of the criticisms have a certain amount of justification. I feel now

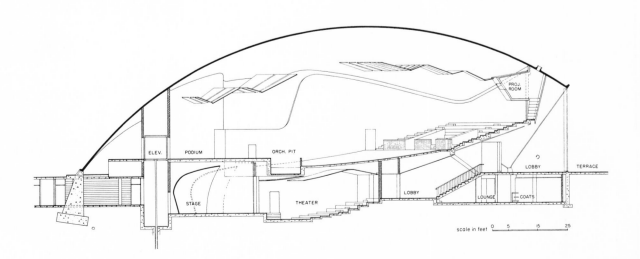

that the building is not enough of a lifting form and that perhaps it does lack sufficient definition of scale. Our belief in the effectiveness of the interior shape and space and in the good acoustics has been justified.

The chapel presented quite a different problem. After many experiments, exploring different shapes in the site plan, the round cylindrical form seemed right. This circular shape also seemed right in plan – for this was basically a chapel where the individual could come and pray and he would be in intimate contact with the altar.

It seemed right to use a traditional material, such as brick, for the chapel – for brick would be a contrast to the auditorium and yet the same material as the surrounding dormitories. But we felt that brick should be used with the same principles of integrity to material as concrete or steel. This is forthrightly a brick structure.

The challenge of the interior was to create an atmosphere conducive to individual prayer. Since this is, uniquely, a non-denominational chapel, it was essential to create an atmosphere which was not derived from a particular religion, but from basic spiritual feelings. A dark interior seemed right – an interior completely separated from the outside world (to which the narthex passage would serve as a sort of decompression chamber). I have always remembered one night on my travels as a student when I sat in a mountain village in Sparta. There was bright moonlight over head and then there was a soft, hushed secondary light around the horizon. That sort of bilateral lighting seemed best to achieve this other-worldly sense. Thus, the central light would come from above the altar – dramatized by the shimmering golden screen by Harry Bertoia – and the secondary light would be light reflected up from the surrounding moat through the arches.

The interior wall was curved, both for acoustical reasons, and to give the space a lack of sharp definition and an increased sense of turning inward. The arches on the outside occur where the exterior wall and the undulating interior wall meet. In retrospect, especially after having looked again at the archivolts of Romanesque churches, I wish that we had given these arches a richer, stronger three-dimensional quality. And I am aware that the connection between narthex and chapel is clumsy. However, I am happy with the interior of the chapel. I think we managed to make it a place where an individual can contemplate things larger than himself.

We made many designs searching for the right form and the right proportion for the bell-tower. I believe that the architect has to determine the basic form and mass and scale of such elements. But since such a spire was really something halfway between architecture and sculpture, we felt that a sculptor who would be sympathetic to the architectural problem as we saw it could bring to the spire a special sensitivity. I think Theodore Roszak has done this job extremely well. [January, 1959]

Looking back at this early work, I think the dome and chapel can be criticized as being too egocentric. The shapes of the buildings are closed. They do not contribute anything toward creating unity within an area which so badly needs unity. From the beginning, we conceived of these buildings on a great square, but neglected to define and crystallize exactly how it would be achieved. This we should have done.

I am delighted that M.I.T. now has building plans in which I hope to have the opportunity of correcting this error. And my hopes are that we will be able to create a large court where we can pull all of the surrounding buildings together into one homogeneous whole – in a sense continue the spirit of the Welles Bosworth buildings at M.I.T. – not in the actual architecture, but in the largeness of spirit. [*Architectural Record*, November, 1960]

THE WEEKEND I WILL SPEND
WITH WIRE & PLASTOSINE
AND MAKE MANY ALTERNATIVES
FOR JIMMIE (MODEL SHOP)(SMITH)
TO MAKE IN MORE PERMANENT
FORM.

DO YOU THINK IT
IS GETTING TOO
COMPLICATED?
REMENICENT?

BASICALLY I THINK THESE
FORMS ARE RIGHT BUT
IT LOOKS A BIT SWEET
AND CHINOISERIE AND
SWEDISH OF THE 20 TIES

THIS THING I LIKE
WITH THE BELL BELOW

I STILL HAVE TO
THINK ABOUT
THIS ONE

THIS ONE IN FRONT

THIS IS NOT RIGHT YET BUT SOMEHOW I THINK
THE UNSYMETRICALITY UP TO A CERTAIN POINT
IS RIGHT HERE AND TO IT I AM TRYING TO
SEE TO WHAT DEGREE.

The site of the War Memorial Center is a bridgehead extending beyond a forty-foot bluff. The building was to be a monument in its own right. It was also to act as a gateway to the park which extends below the bluff down to Lake Michigan and to make a transition between city and lakeside park.

Fulfilling its complicated program, the building consists of three parts. One is the base, which builds the mass up to the city level and contains an art museum; the second, on city level, is the memorial court with a pool. The names of the war dead are inscribed around it. The court is surrounded by the polyhedron-shaped piers which support the building and also make frames for the breathtaking views of lake and sky. The third part is the superstructure, cantilevered outward thirty feet in three directions, which contains the meeting halls and offices of the veterans' organizations. The vertical and horizontal structural walls of this cantilevered superstructure form box-like rectangles, open on the outer sides.

One of the greatest challenges was to create a building, comparatively small in size on a comparatively small site, which would assert itself as an important building and would proclaim itself as a monumental building which could hold its own against the vast panorama of lake and sky. I think we succeeded in achieving this affirmative quality by making a concrete building with bold cantilevers which is always and in all parts and in every aspect of its structure a wholly concrete building.

It is a concrete structure where the structure is contained within its box-kite-like shape. It differs from any vaulted or plastic form concrete, but it is a structure where every plane, whether vertical or horizontal, is a working part of the total structure. The building and finishes are rough. It is not a refined building, nor is any part of it hesitant or reticent. It depends for monumentality and dignity on the clarity of its structure, on its 'guts' and its simplicity.

From the beginning, we had thought of the concrete walls or panels within the box-like rectangle of the front elevation being covered with some smooth, shiny material, so that this non-structural wall would contrast both in texture and color with the structural concrete frame and walls and would be an element of particular beauty. We thought of this as an enriching surface, primarily monochromatic in tone, which would neither compete with nor dominate the structural expression. We were pleased that the commission for such a mosaic was given to the Wisconsin artist, Edmund Lewandowski. [January, 1959]

I am interested that you write you think I will make my big contribution in concrete. It is a material which is beginning to interest me more and more. It presents many challenges as well as many opportunities. It seemed the inevitable material for the Milwaukee building. I suppose someday it will even prove to be competitive with steel for high-rise buildings. [To a journalist, May 5, 1953]

Looking back, I wish that the staircases in the court and all parts of the interiors had been given the same qualities of 'guts' and boldness as the building itself. Yes, I think the building is strong enough to carry them, but they would have been better if they were what Wright would call 'organic' parts. [To a friend, June, 1961]

Our concern was the creation of an architecture which would support and express the idea of this particular college. We wanted to create an environment appropriate to the intellectual and spiritual training of young men who would go on to professional studies in theology.

The strategic question was the relation of the buildings to the world. On the one hand, we all felt that they should not be inward-turning and removed like medieval monasteries; but, on the other hand, we felt the group must – for its purpose – have a tranquil atmosphere of at least partial self-sufficiency. The solution seemed to lie in the village-concept: a group of buildings which would have a quiet, unified environment into which the students could withdraw to find a complete, balanced life and yet one which was related to the outside world.

In a village of the North European type, the chapel is placed in the center, on the highest spot, an all-important symbol around which the other buildings are grouped. In a careful study of this site, we found we could use a little hill next to the valley (which is now the lake) as the heart of the campus. We could put the chapel here, to dominate the entire group and to be reflected in the lake below.

The pitched roof seemed to give the right architectural character to the whole complex. This sort of roof is symbolic of the North European church. By using it on all the buildings, we could unite the group in one spirit. By making the pitch of the roofs on the other buildings lower than on the chapel, the lesser buildings would seem to rise upward to the most significant one. Since the group would be seen not only from within the complex but from across the fields as well, the silhouette was an important consideration. The village-like cluster with the varied lines of pitched roofs seemed to make a pleasing, expressive silhouette. We tried to achieve further unity by careful attention to the site-plan and by the consistent use of brick walls and black-tiled roofs.

The chapel was, of course, the building that required the most thought and imagination. This is the building where spiritual values are epitomized and these are the hardest qualities to express in brick and mortar. We realized that light is an effective agent in creating a spiritual atmosphere. We used very low lighting from the side walls as well as lighting from above to get the restful, balanced quality we sought. Additional side windows dramatized the altar as a focal point.

We wanted to work with the simple chapel shape appropriate to the Lutheran church and to create an interior in which the relationship of human beings to enclosed space would be appropriate and inspiring. The problem was also to find a shape and materials which would allow the spoken word to be heard clearly and one in which the organ could swell to its fullest. We believe the high chapel interior answered these requirements.

In housing these pre-ministry students, we wanted to make the greatest impact upon them with the least expenditure. By extremely careful utilization of every square foot, we reached a desirable end: groups of thirty-six students live together on staggered floors in buildings which are no bigger than a large house. We hoped that this intimate housing would encourage real student responsibility for the group within each house. [April, 1958]

I wish we had carried the simple, rugged character more forcefully, vigorously, and consistently into all interiors and detailing. [May, 1960]

The U. S. Chancellery on Grosvenor Square is a very simple, symmetrical building designed to fit with this symmetrical square.

At one time, the dominant characteristic of Grosvenor Square was low rowhouses in a variety of styles and motifs, packed so closely next to each other that they became a unified frame. But the Grosvenor Estate, which controls the square, has a new master plan, whereby three sides of the square will form one large pseudo-Georgian composition. These buildings, with a uniform cornice line, red brick walls, Portland cement columns and balustrades, etc., will give the square a new aspect. It is for this future square – not the one that exists only in people's memories – that the embassy building, the fourth side of this giant outdoor room, was designed.

It was important that the embassy building be harmonious with the square, but it also had to be a proud building in its own right, for an embassy building is an important building both to the host country and the guest country and, therefore, I believe it should be a landmark.

We sought harmony in various ways. The mass and general cornice height – the silhouette against the sky – conform to those of the buildings in the future square. There is continuity of material: the Portland stone which is trim and ornament on the red brick pseudo-Georgian buildings becomes *the* material for the embassy. When the Portland stone on the new building darkens to the same tone as that on the surrounding edifices, this continuity will be clearly seen. Portland stone seemed appropriate, too, since it is the material generally used on official buildings in London. It is a stone, moreover, which – if used with broken surfaces – gains with time a beautiful pattern and texture of whites and blacks. We knew that if we gave the wall sufficient texture of in and out surfaces, time and London soot and rain and wind would make this a dramatically dark building.

There is a general scale set up by the size of windows and decorations on the pseudo-Georgian façades. The same scale, only slightly bolder, has been sought in the embassy façade by the structural system that forms it. This wall structure of coupled precast concrete columns placed alternately above each other creates a fenestration that is related to that of the other buildings. This structural system also gave the desired plastic quality.

The façade one sees is the bones of the building. The coupled columns (precast frames) on the upper floors carry all the weight (floors, etc.) down to the outer edge of the diagrid; this diagrid transfers the load horizontally to the first floor columns.

The Consulate and U. S. Information Service have entrances on side streets. As the most important, the embassy functions have their entrance on Grosvenor Square. To enhance this entrance, there are three free-standing columns and, directly above, like a pediment, is the eagle of the United States. Here the eagle is used not in the form of the Great Seal (which appears inside the entrance doors), but freely and symbolically as it has so often been used in the past. (I wish its wingspread had been a couple of feet longer.) Public functions are housed on the two lower floors; the more private embassy ones are located above. This functional separation is made clear in the design.

Through choice of materials and the character of the architecture, we tried to create a stateliness and formality which would express the meaning of the building. I believe we achieved a completely integrated relationship between the inside and the outside and that our detailing on the interior carries through the theme of the outside completely. [June 15, 1960]

In my own mind, the building is much better than the English think – but not quite as good as I wished it to be. [August 4, 1961]

U.S. Embassy Chancellery
Oslo, Norway
1955–1959

The triangular shape of the U. S. Chancellery in Oslo was inevitable. The site is a triangular block, with streets on three sides. The main façade is on Drammensveien, one of the principal streets of Oslo. It faces the Royal Palace, which is set in spacious, park-like gardens. The character of Drammensveien is of continuous façades and it seemed important not to break this continuity. Therefore, our main façade respects the Drammensveien building line. The side façades follow the line of the side streets. Trees will link them to the greenery of the Palace gardens.

In a sense, the building is conceived as a triangular Renaissance palace, with rooms surrounding a court. However, the climate of Oslo demanded that this court be enclosed and skylighted, rather than open. Moreover, since for many months the grey, cold weather demands a completely interior civilization, it seemed wise to give the court a feeling of warmth and enclosure. Hence, the warm beige Roman travertine floor, the teakwood walls, and the brick grille. The diamond shape of the court is a natural result of the triangular plan. It is a triangle with two corners taken out for stairways, elevators, utilities, etc. In the center of the court is a pool, for which we planned a fifteen-foot-high sculpture to accent the volume of the court. We are hoping this will come to pass. Warm lighting in the court gives a feeling of sunshine in this city which is sunless for many months.

The precast façade is the most interesting and successful part of this building. Our attempt was to integrate the module, on which the offices are all based, with the structural system, so that we could conceive, all in one, a precast modular structural system with an integrated façade material. These precast units have an integral surface, consisting of ninety per cent of Norwegian emerald pearl granite polished.

Precasting had not advanced as far in Norway as in the neighboring countries of Sweden and Denmark. But a superb job was done here with the help of experts from these other Scandinavian countries and from Germany. A magnificent building material was created and a new industry was started for Norway. The material has a rich, dark green color and an inherent luster. It gives the façade a changing sheen and a vitality which are uncommon in precast walls. The three-dimensional quality of the wall, which is derived from its basic structural shape, enhances these qualities. As one walks along Drammensveien, these structural units seem to become a changing checkerboard of mat and shiny, light and dark surfaces. [March, 1959]

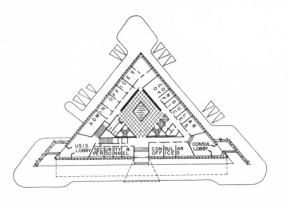

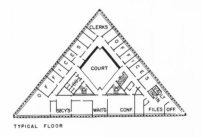

TYPICAL FLOOR

52

I believe the David S. Ingalls Hockey Rink is one of the best buildings we have done and I am very proud of it.

The concept of the building was arrived at as a completely logical consequence of the problem. There was the site – an open location, somewhat remote from the compact campus. It seemed a place where one could express the special nature of this absolutely independent building and could express its structure freely. The site indicated that the building should be placed in such a way that its entrance was at the end closest to the campus.

There was the functional requirement: a hockey rink of standard size (eighty-five by 200 feet) with seating for 2,800 (and the possibility for 5,000 when the rink would be used for other purposes). These requirements indicated a stadium-like plan, roughly oval in shape, with access corridors or ramps around the seating area.

The question was how best to span this area. With the structural engineer, Fred Severud, we worked out a system of a central arch spanning the length of the rink and a hanging roof coming down from this arch.

The great spine-like concrete arch is the dominant theme. We wanted it to be both structurally effective and beautiful. We decided to counteract the normally downward aspect of the arch form by making the ends sweep up in cantilevered extensions. This soaring form was further emphasized by the lighting fixture at the entrance end, which we commissioned from a sculptor, Oliver Andrews, so it would have expressive as well as functional meaning.

The cables, which were suspended in catenary curves from the central arch, stretch down to their anchorage in the exterior walls on each side. These curved walls are counterparts to the arch: they are in plan as the shape of the center arch is in section. These walls, which surround the scooped-out stadium, were also made to slope, both in order to increase structural efficiency and to enhance the visual expression of the stress flows. Vaulted or domed shapes often have a heaviness or bulginess. On this exterior, the contrast of the concave and the convex seem to me to have achieved the kind of sweep and lightness which we wanted.

The interior is absolutely simple. The wood deck of the roof really looks like boat construction. The structural members are visible – the sweeping arch and the longitudinal cables under the roof. The concrete, the wood, the ice, and the fluorescent lights all seem in character with each other. They seem to me to give a luminosity and lightness to the interior space which make one almost feel as if one were floating.

It is a building which, as Severud has said, expresses in its various forms and in the ways its materials are used the tug-of-war between pull and resistance. It is a building in which the form-world created by the basic ingredients of the structure is carried out in all the component parts. And it is a building in which we have not hesitated to dramatize and emphasize. Thus, in summary, I would say that I think the building succeeded because of the clarity and strength of its statement and because of the consistency and relatedness of all its parts. [January, 1959]

I like the story of the boy on the Yale team who said when he looked up at the concrete arch, it made him feel 'Go, go, go!' [To a friend, April, 1960]

Yes, I would agree the Hockey Rink marks an important moment in my work. You could say it strengthened my convictions about making everything part of the same 'form-world' and gave us confidence about handling vaults and suspended roofs – which have interested me since some projects of the 'Fifties and the Aspen tent. It influenced both TWA and the Washington airport. I think that the critics have tended to underestimate the hockey rink. [To a friend, June 6, 1961]

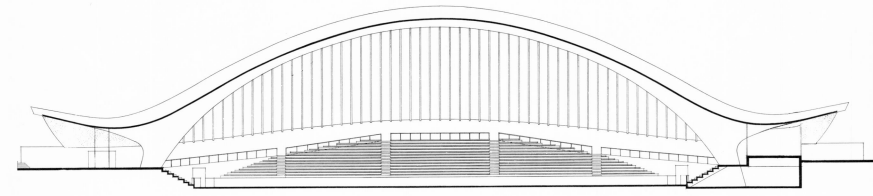

LONGITUDINAL   SECTION

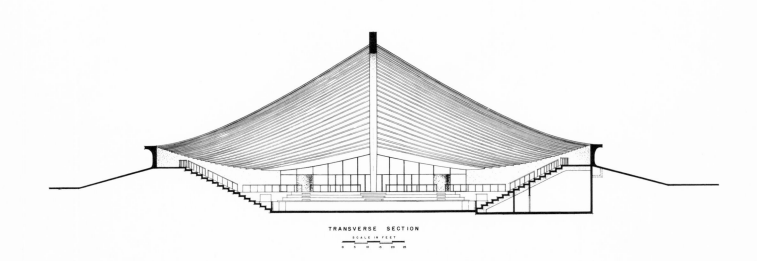

TRANSVERSE   SECTION

SCALE IN FEET

0    5    10    15    20    25

The challenge of the Trans World Airlines terminal was twofold. One, to create, within the complex of terminals that makes up Idlewild, a building for TWA which would be distinctive and memorable. Its particular site – directly opposite Idlewild's main entrance road and at the apex of the curve in the far end of the terminal complex – gave us the opportunity of designing a building which could relate to the surrounding buildings in mass, but still assert itself as a dramatic accent.

Two, to design a building in which the architecture itself would express the drama and specialness and excitement of travel. Thus, we wanted the architecture to reveal the terminal, not as a static, enclosed place, but as a place of movement and of transition.

Therefore, we arrived at this structure, which consists essentially of four interacting barrel vaults of slightly different shapes, supported on four Y-shaped columns. Together, these vaults make a vast concrete shell, fifty feet high and 315 feet long, which makes a huge umbrella over all the passenger areas. The shapes of these vaults were deliberately chosen in order to emphasize an upward-soaring quality of line, rather than the downward gravitational one common to many domed structures. We wanted to counteract the earthbound feeling and the heaviness that prevails too much in the M.I.T. auditorium. We wanted an uplift. For the same reason, the structural shapes of the columns were dramatized to stress their upward-curving sweep. The bands of skylights, which separate and articulate the four vaults, increase the sense of airiness and lightness.

In studying the problem in model after model, both exterior and interior, we realized that having determined on this basic form for the vaulting, we had committed ourselves to a family of forms and must carry the same integral character throughout the entire building. All the curvatures, all the spaces and elements, down to the shapes of signs, information boards, railings, and counters, would have to have one consistent character. As the passenger walked through the sequence of the building, we wanted him to be in a total environment where each part was the consequence of another and all belonged to the same form-world. It is our strong belief that only through such a consistency and such a consequential development can a building make its fullest impact and expression. [January, 1959]

That's right, the Baroque architects were wrestling with the same problem of creating dynamic space. Within the limits of the classical order and their technology, they were trying to see how far they could go into a non-static architecture. At TWA, we tried to take the discipline imposed by the concrete shell vault and give it this non-static quality. In a sense, we were doing the same thing, but using different play-blocks. [*Horizon*, July, 1960]

The fact that to some people it looked like a bird in flight was really coincidental. That was the last thing we ever thought about. Now, that doesn't mean that one doesn't have the right to see it that way or to explain it to laymen in those terms, especially because laymen are usually more literally than visually inclined. [*Horizon* interview, June 19, 1959]

TWA is beginning to look marvelous. If anything happened and they had to stop work right now and just leave it in this state, I think it would make a beautiful ruin, like the Baths of Caracalla. [After his last visit to the site, when only the concrete vaults had been completed, April 17, 1961]

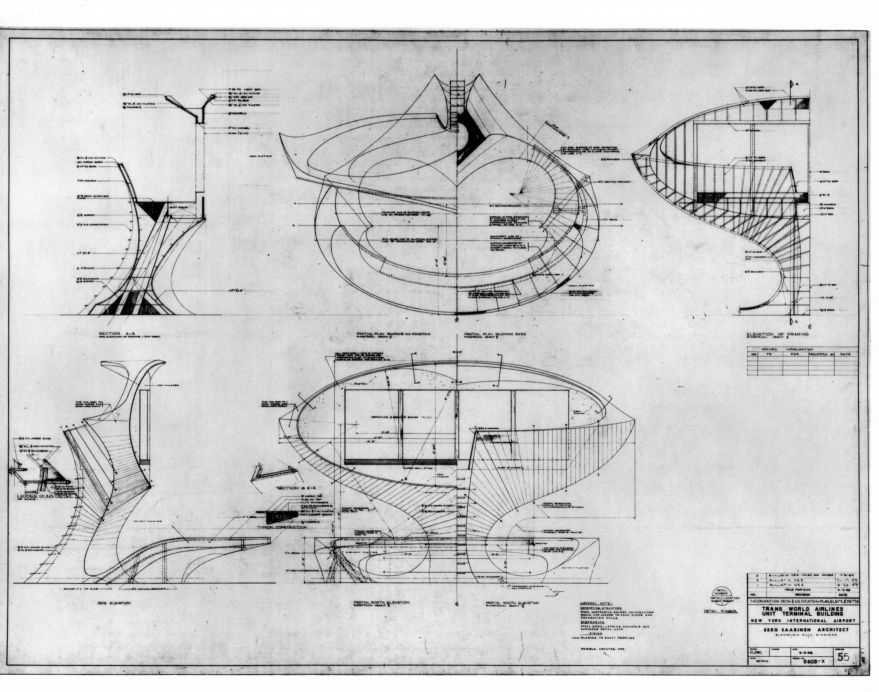

I believe very strongly that the whole field of design is all one thing. Therefore, my interest in furniture. [To a friend, December 6, 1948]

Though we use mass-produced parts in architecture, a building is custom-built to the extent it is a solution of a specific problem. In furniture design, the client is Everyman. [*Architectural Design*, August 1957]

The chair is a three-dimensional object always seen within a room, which is essentially a box. How do you best relate this object to the box? The cubists, the de Stijl designers, Mies van der Rohe, and Le Corbusier all saw this fundamental relationship and solved it by their light steel furniture – truly beautiful thinking and truly beautiful furniture. Somehow technology and taste have shifted. New materials and techniques have given us great opportunities with structural shells of plywood, plastic and metal. For me, the compound shell of plastic is most appropriate for twentieth-century furniture. The problem then becomes a sculptural one, not the cubist, constructivist one. [*passim*, 1949 to 1960]

I designed the 'womb' chair because there seemed to be a need for a large and really comfortable chair to take the place of the old overstuffed chair. These dreadnoughts disappeared from modern interiors, partly because they were designed for an era which tried to impress by sheer mass, partly because their manufacture depended upon hundreds of hand-labor operations and costs became too high. But the need for such chairs has not passed. Today, more than ever before, we need to relax.

In arriving at the design, there were many problems which had to be recognized. First, there is the fact that people sit differently today than in the Victorian era. They want to sit lower and they like to slouch. In my first post-war chair, I attempted to shape the slouch in an organized way by giving support for the back as well as the seat, shoulders and head. The 'womb' chair also has three planes of support.

Then, there is the fact that a comfortable position, even if it were the most comfortable in the world, would not be so for very long. The necessity of changing one's position is an important factor often forgotten in chair design. So, too, is the fact that an equal distribution of weight over a large surface of the body is important.

The 'womb' chair also attempts to achieve a psychological comfort by providing a great big cup-like shell into which you can curl up and pull up your legs (something which women seem especially to like to do). A chair is a background for a person sitting in it. Thus, the chair should not only look well as a piece of sculpture in the room when no one is in it, it should also be a flattering background when someone is in it – especially the female occupant.

The scale of the chair was thought of as having architectural value. This larger form could make a transition to the loose furnishings. [*passim*, 1947 to 1957]

As to the pedestal furniture. The undercarriage of chairs and tables in a typical interior makes an ugly, confusing, unrestful world. I wanted to clear up the slum of legs. I wanted to make the chair all one thing again. All the great furniture of the past from Tutankhamun's chair to Thomas Chippendale's have always been a structural total. With our excitement over plastic and plywood shells, we grew away from this structural total. As now manufactured, the pedestal furniture is half-plastic, half-metal. I look forward to the day when the plastic industry has advanced to the point where the chair will be one material, as designed. [*passim*, 1958]

The architectural challenge in designing this research center seemed to be that of reconciling two apparently contradictory requirements. We wanted to make the laboratories and research offices the most efficient and flexible of twentieth-century research centers. We also wanted an expression for the building that would be appropriate to the personality of the users and the site and the environment.

First, the laboratories. An investigation of what had been happening in laboratory and office planning brought out several new facts which had to be recognized. One new fact was the increasing demand for concentration, for a compact building with short communication lines and utmost privacy for small groups of scientists. Another fact was that the expanding needs of research and its yet unknown frontiers made flexibility of space and arrangements more important than ever before. Of primary significance was the realization that laboratories and offices today depend on air conditioning and on efficient fluorescent lighting rather than on windows for their ventilation and lighting.

All these considerations led us to a radically new plan for research centers for our time. In this plan, all laboratories and offices are put in interior space and the window-periphery is left for the main corridors.

In the Thomas J. Watson Research Center, the cross-corridors, on which the laboratories and offices are located, are only about 120 feet long. The laboratories are placed back to back, with the laboratory utility core between them. Likewise, the offices are placed back to back, with a specially designed modular storage system for files, supplies, costs, etc., in the wall between. These short cross-corridors are joined by two trunk corridors which run uninterruptedly along each side of the 1,090-foot-long building. The trunk corridor on the north (or front) side is totally of glass; on the south, it is of glass and stone. (We have used this new basic plan in a much larger and more formal scheme for the Bell Telephone Laboratories at Holmdel, New Jersey, and believe it has wide possibilities.)

The human and economic advantages of this plan are many. It provides the desired concentration, privacy, flexibility, and easy communication lines. It saves laboratory utility costs. By reducing outside walls, it reduces the overall costs. It allows the best controlled environment for each individual. Instead of small windows in offices and laboratories covered with view-obscuring sun-screening devices, the floor-to-ceiling windows on the main corridors can be uncovered like open galleries. They present an unobstructed view of the very beautiful landscape and provide a real encounter with nature at the moments of relaxation when one has left office or laboratory and can truly appreciate and enjoy it.

Now, to the other problem: the character of the building and its relation to its site. It has always seemed to me that many scientists in the research field are like university professors – tweedy, pipe-smoking men. We wanted to provide them with a relaxed, 'tweedy,' outdoor environment as a deliberate contrast to the efficient, precise laboratories and offices.

The beautifully hilly site and the landscape with its characteristic fieldstone walls encouraged this aim. We knew also that IBM was anxious to have a center which would not be architecturally obnoxious to its neighbors.

All these considerations led us to the use of local stone, Westchester fieldstone, much of which actually came from the site. We used it on the end walls of the build-

ing as well as on the inner side of the peripheral corridors and on the lobby, auditorium, and cafeteria walls.

The building was curved in a crescent, following the configuration of the hill. It is planned so that this curve can embrace the hill even further by extending the crescent in its future expansion. I think it looks well wedded to its site and that the crescent form gives nice, changing aspects.

The building is three-storeyed, but it appears variously as a one-, or a two-, or a three-storey building, depending on the point from which it is viewed. From the main access drive, sweeping across the main, or north front, the building appears as a three-storey structure. If one approaches it from the parking lot, at the back or south side, one walks on a bridge over a Japanese garden designed by Sasaki, Walker, & Associates. One sees the building then as a one-storey structure and enters on the third floor. If one comes in from the garden below, one sees a two-storey building and enters it on the second floor.

The driveway forms a crescent shape, a small, tangential counterpart to the arc-shape of the building. This curving shape, with the marquee at the center, is emphasized by long, raking fieldstone walls. The end of each of these is accented with a sculpture commissioned from Seymour Lipton. These two nine-foot-long sculptures, of nickel-silver on Monel metal, are called *Argonaut I* and *Argonaut II*, referring to the heroes on the ship *Argos*, who set out in search of the Golden Fleece. To the sculptor, the quest parallels the scientists' search into the unknown for something mysteriously ideal. Their form is congruent with the curved space and the curved walls and they suggest motion, even flight.

I am very happy with these sculptures. Their silvery-gold looks handsome against the dark background of the building. Beautiful in themselves, they are splendid in their architectural relationships.

Another commissioned work of art is the bronze head of the late Thomas J. Watson by Jacques Lipchitz, which the visitor sees as he enters the auditorium. I think it is strong and successful. [April 17, 1961]

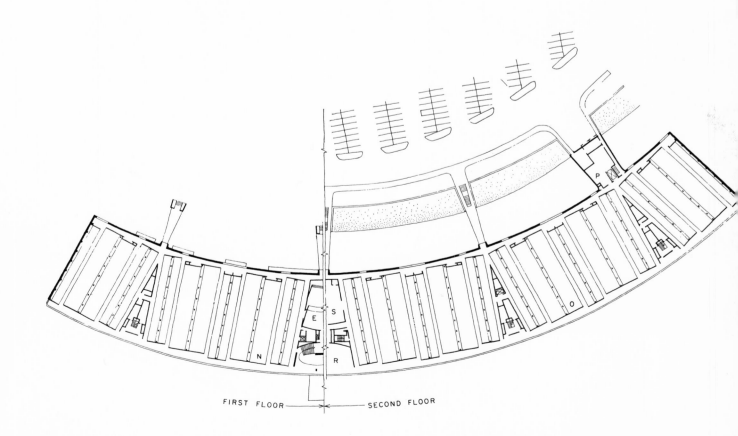

FIRST FLOOR — SECOND FLOOR

The architectural character was determined largely by the site and the character of the company. The 600-acre site consists both of high table land and low river land, its edges broken by wooded ravines. One of the broad ravines seemed the finest, most pleasant and most human site for the building complex. In such a tree-studded site, where it would be intimately connected with nature, a strong, dark building seemed appropriate.

Deere & Co. is a secure, well-established, successful farm machinery company, proud of its Midwestern farm-belt location. Farm machinery is not slick, shiny metal but forged iron and steel in big, forceful, functional shapes. The proper character for its headquarters' architecture should likewise not be a slick, precise, glittering glass and spindly metal building, but a building which is bold and direct, using metal in a strong, basic way.

Having decided to use steel, we wanted to make a steel building that was *really* a steel building (most so-called steel buildings seem to me to be more glass buildings than steel buildings, really not one thing or the other). We sought for an appropriate material – economical, maintenance free, bold in character, dark in color. We located a certain high tensile steel, which has a peculiar characteristic: if this steel is left unpainted, a rust coating forms which becomes a protective skin over the steel. This rust coating – which does not develop beyond a certain point – is a cinnamon-brown color which makes a beautiful dark surface on the steel. We built a full-size mock-up section of the façade on the site to make sure the steel would act as we had anticipated. It has. I predict other architects will use it widely.

The plan was determined both by the client's needs and the site. The eight-storey administration building is placed crosswise on the floor of the valley. At its fourth floor level, glass-enclosed flying bridges stretch out to the laboratory and the exhibition buildings on the high slopes of the ravine. The complex is approached from the valley below. We planned the roads carefully, keeping in mind how the building would be seen as one drove along the man-made lake up to the parking lot behind the building and to the entrance.

Having selected a site because of the beauty of nature, we were especially anxious to take full advantage of views from the offices. To avoid curtains or Venetian blinds, which would obscure the views, we worked out a system of sun-shading with metal louvers and specified reflective glass to prevent glare. These louvers will cut out direct sun about ninety per cent of the time. We were not trying to ignore the fact that a sun problem will exist for some nice, sunny days in winter. I know the problem is there and one must face it. But we felt it was more important to retain the open quality of the design, which could be enjoyed *without* sun problems for ninety per cent of the year, than to sacrifice it for a small amount of time. We will solve the sun problem that will exist occasionally for some of the offices in winter in some positive but modest way.

Besides functioning as an efficient sun-shading device, the steel louvers dramatize the character of the building, which is one where we have tried to use steel to express strength. [*passim*, August, 1957–June, 1961]

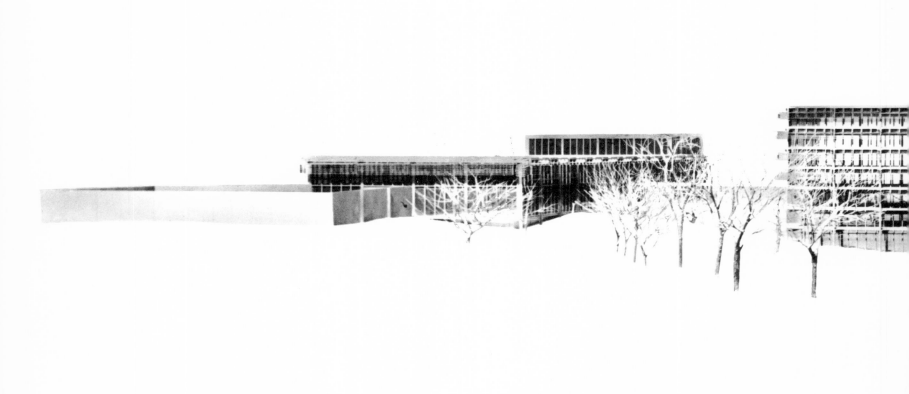

Almost all architectural problems can be solved within the general framework and vernacular of modern architecture. But sometimes, as in these new colleges for Yale, a special problem poses a special challenge.

These two new colleges are to be placed in the shadow, on one side, of the pseudo-Gothic gymnasium with its formidable scale, and, on the other, of the pseudo-Gothic graduate school with its somewhat smaller scale. The site is angular and odd. Thus, the relationship of the new buildings to their neighbors and to the difficult site was one part of this special challenge.

But another part was the spirit and meaning of the colleges. Somehow, the architecture had to declare them as *colleges*, not as dormitories. The more we studied and thought about their function and purpose, the more convinced we became that their emphasis as colleges must be clearly on the individual as an individual, not as an anonymous integer in a group.

Talks with students strengthened our belief that the rooms should be as individual as possible, as random as those in an old inn rather than as standardized as those in a modern motel. Instead of finding a system and fitting everyone into it, we should try to start with the idea of diversity – of many different rooms, rooms in towers, rooms of varying shapes and sizes and kinds, with various window and study arrangements. The University's decision that the great majority of rooms should be single rooms confirmed this idea of the importance of the individual.

Of our time, but also timeless, the architecture should show that these colleges were worlds somewhat apart, worlds with their own flavor, with emphasis on the individual and his scholarly life. In every part, from students' and public rooms to the self-contained environment of the courts and the building materials themselves, the architecture must express the specialness of these colleges. The architecture must keep them, too, from looking like poor cousins in comparison to the existing colleges, which have all the luxuries that were possible in the earlier periods when building costs were one-third what they are today and the budget allotment per student exactly what it is today.

We realized that these very special problems could not be solved within the general current vocabulary of modern architecture, which seemed at absolute variance with what we should be achieving. Repetition, regularity, uniformity, standardization – all prime parts of the vernacular – were at direct odds with the diversity, variety and individuality we wanted. Flatness, lightness, glistening aluminum and glass, smoothness instead of rough texture and play of light and shade could all, likewise, neither express the spirit we wanted nor be compatible with our neighboring buildings. An architecture of rectangles and cubes seemed ill-suited, too, to this site, where practically no two angles are the same and the abutting buildings were all at vastly different angles.

We became convinced we would have to create a new vocabulary or add to the vocabulary of modern architecture in order to find a solution.

What have we done? We have made the buildings polygonal – their shapes derived in order to provide the special and diverse student rooms, to answer the needs of the site and to give variety and sequence of spatial experiences in the courts. We have used a large-scale bending of walls back and forth to give these buildings a scale that would make them stand up next to the surrounding buildings. Most significantly, we conceived of these colleges as citadels of earthy, monolithic masonry

PAYNE WHITNEY GYMNASIUM (EXISTING)

TOWER           MORSE
MASTER'S HOUSE

GRADUATE
SCHOOL
(EXISTING)

Photo
page 86

# M O R S E   C O L L E G E

Photo
page 83

MORSE DINING HALL

Photo
page 87

EZRA STILES DINING HALL

# E Z R A   S T I L E S   C O L L E G E

Photo
page
85

T O W E R   P A R K W A Y

EZRA STILES
MASTER'S HOUSE      TOWER

YALE CO-OP STORE

B R O A D W A Y

– buildings where masonry walls would be dominant and whose interiors of stone, oak, and plaster would carry out the spirit of strength and simplicity.

One of the reasons the general vocabulary of modern architecture does not usually include masonry walls is that these require handicraft methods which are anachronistic. But we found a new technological method for making these walls (and we tried it out in a nine-foot-high sample). These are masonry walls made without masons, masonry walls which are 'modern.'

Evolving a new kind of architectural vocabulary is not a simple problem. Idea, site, plan, and structural system all have to be pulled together into one thing – into an architecture. Months and months of trial and error and again more trial and error were involved. Each decision altered every aspect of the design. For instance, there were many dozens of studies of windows – their placement and proportion, their framing and bases, the way they worked in plan, the way they looked in elevation. Putting windows in this kind of a monolithic masonry wall in buildings which were polygonal in plan was in all ways a new problem.

Through this slow process, gradually 'do's' and 'don'ts' evolve. Gradually, these become convictions. Eventually, one learns a grammar of forms and shapes that fit together and work with the new material and surroundings. I look upon this architecture that has evolved under these special conditions as an architecture with certain truths and one which answers certain needs of our time that are more widespread than this one-time use. I believe there are many potentials and developments inherent in this polygonal masonry architecture. I want to explore them.

As for the site plan: in this area the plan for Yale and the whole city plan of New Haven are interlocked. In the master planning of the area, it seemed desirable to find a solution which would work well with Tower Parkway remaining as an awkward thoroughfare through the area, but would work even better were the city in the future to build a circumferential highway and to close Tower Parkway. The plan that seemed to have the greatest potential and give the best setting for the tremendous Payne-Whitney gym is a great, roughly crescent-shaped plaza in front of the gymnasium. If and when Tower Parkway were closed, there would be the possibility of placing a third college so that it would complete the sweeping arc.

It is economically desirable to have a common kitchen for the two colleges. We took advantage of that fact by placing the kitchen under a narrow, winding walk, not unlike a small Italian hilltown street, with its steps going up and down and its balconies projecting. Students using the street going to and from the gym will enjoy a variety of visual experiences.

One of the most beautiful elements in the existing colleges at Yale is the courts. The courts of the new colleges, varied in levels and terraces, surrounded by their polygonal buildings, will create in new terms these desirable and changing interior-exterior spaces. Since other colleges at Yale have some kind of tower or belfry to identify themselves in the silhouette of the city, it seemed right that these two colleges should also raise their heads high. Therefore, the two towers were made a part of the general composition. [November 4, 1959]

The colleges are looking strong, as I hoped they would, and they really work with the other buildings. We must plant ivy as soon as possible and decide on a sculptor for the dining-hall chandeliers. [August 11, 1961]

Let me explain a little of my thinking about the problem of designing a new church for the Disciples of Christ in Columbus. I think we have to face first some of the problems of what has been happening in America today with the church and religion and architecture.

In the eleventh-twelfth centuries, there was the cathedral and it was the significant thing. Maybe it had a cloisters or a priory or some little low building off to the side, but the cathedral building itself dominated everything. Today, there are Sunday school rooms and good-fellowship rooms and kitchens and gymnasiums and square dancing rooms and so forth. All these have tended to sprout into separate buildings and to get bigger and bigger and more and more important and finally, the church itself has become an insignificant, almost forgotten little thing.

So, in this church, I would like to put all that activity downstairs. Maybe underground, hidden away, and put only the sanctuary above ground and make it the significant visual and architectural thing.

Then, congregations and church building committees always want the architect to make everything on one level and easy, sort of inviting you to come in like a supermarket. But I don't think religion should be something easy. I think you should have to work for it and it should be a special thing. The architecture should express this. That is an absolutely marvelous experience at Borobudur and at Angkor Wat, when you keep climbing those steep steps and all the time are being subjected by the architecture to awarenesses of special and spiritual qualities.

So, I think this sanctuary should be elevated and make you climb up to it. There is another reason why this church must be elevated and that is the site. It is a flat site in a residential district. The church must be elevated so that it stands proudly above the parked cars and the surrounding little ranch-type houses and can be seen.

There is another thing about the approach. That has to do with why people go to church. There is Christmas and Easter, but I mean beyond that. I suppose one of the important reasons for going to active worship is to remind themselves about religion and God. Now, this church will have a cemetery connected with it. I think it might be a good idea to place the church in the center of the cemetery. Then every time they came to church, people would have to face up to the stark reality that man is not immortal. Cemeteries can be beautiful places. It could be a very beautiful thing to see a church completely surrounded by a cemetery.

After the approach, there is the act of entering. There should be awareness of a changing environment, like a decompression chamber from the outside world into the church. Maybe you would go down and then up again into the sanctuary. The light, of course, would begin to change, too.

I guess another reason people go actively to church is so they can worship with a group of people of like mind. They will do this in the sanctuary and they should feel they are all in unity and harmony in a special and appropriate spiritual atmosphere.

As I understand the Disciples of Christ, communion is a very important act and the congregation participates in it. The communion table should be the focal point. We can have the congregation sitting all around the communion table where every one feels equal and joined together.

Maybe we can even have a sort of reverse seating – that is, with the seating coming from the bottom and narrowing up toward the center, like a pyramid or a cone,

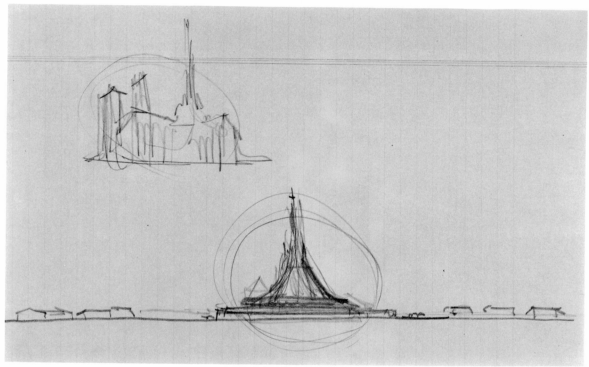

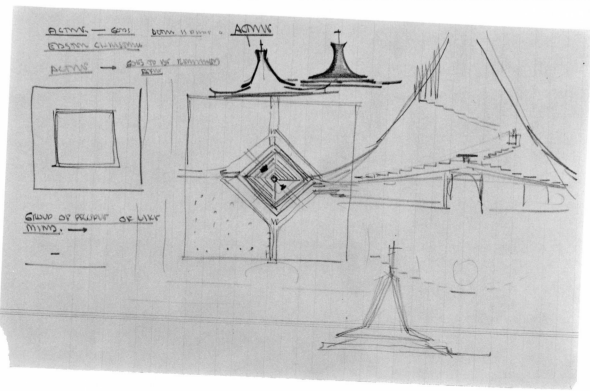

with the communion table at the summit and the pulpit suspended even higher on one side. Every one would then be joined in looking *upward,* instead of down at the back of some one's head. I don't know. We will have to see if that would work with sight lines and circulation of the congregation. It may very well not.

Whatever way we solve that, the congregation should have the positive feeling of being within the church, in a special, enclosed spiritual world. I see it as a very simple interior with the organ pipes an important element in the sanctuary design. The primary element to create the right spiritual atmosphere would, of course, be light. That is the crucial thing.

Now, what form should this church take? If you think of the silhouette of a Christian church, you think first of the tower. Different periods handled the tower, or the spire or the steeple or whatever you want to call it, in different ways. So did we, at Minneapolis and the first Columbus church and m.i.t. and Concordia and so on.

On this site, with this kind of central plan, I think I would like to make the church really all one form: all the tower. There would be the gradual building up of the sheltering, hovering planes becoming the spire. The spire would not be put on a box or come up from the sides of the roof, as we did at Stephens College. The whole thing, all the planes, would grow up organically into the spire.

It would be good as an exterior form, because the spire is a marvelous symbol of reaching upward to God and because it would proclaim this as a church in the silhouette of Columbus. It would also work well as an interior space. It would give a feeling of soaring space and a feeling of special enclosure. It would work well for the light. The primary light source would be an oculus in the spire. It could give intense light on the communion table. This light would lead you in as you saw it from the narthex. It would also keep you from being distracted by the people across from you, but you would be aware of them. Then there could be a feeling of contracting light back in the seating area. And this spire form would work well structurally. The structure could be very simple and would clearly and logically express the form and character of the church. [June, 1960]

As for the baptistery, I feel that should be a small space separate from the nave. The ceremony of total immersion should be given more dignity. It should be viewed only by family and close friends. In the Early Christian church, people were not allowed in the nave until they were baptized and then they were taken in for their first communion. We should have gates between baptistery and sanctuary. [July, 1960]

I know the building committee likes our scheme, but it still isn't right. The problem of the lantern hasn't really been solved. And the inside and the outside aren't really well related. It needs more work. [January 25, 1961]

It would be so easy to say – as you would like me to – 'Let's go ahead with it as it is.' But against that I have perhaps a greater conscience, because I would know in my heart that it would not really be the best I can do.

We have finally to solve this church so that it can become a great building. I feel I have this obligation to the congregation, and as architect I have that obligation to my profession and my ideals. I want to solve it so that as an architect when I face St. Peter I am able to say that out of the buildings I did during my lifetime, one of the best was this little church, because it has in it a real spirit that speaks forth to all Christians as a witness to their faith. [To the client, *April* 18, 1961]

I think we have finally solved the Columbus church. [July 28, 1961]

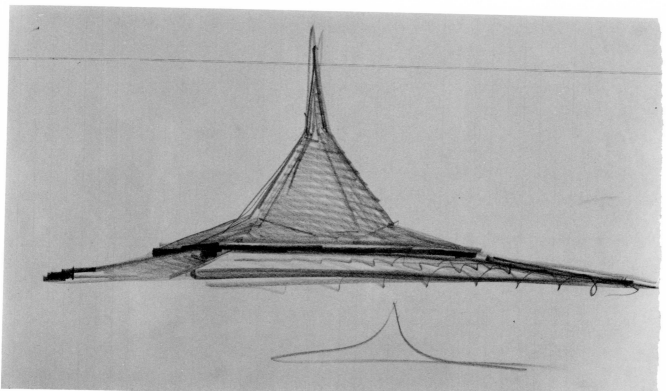

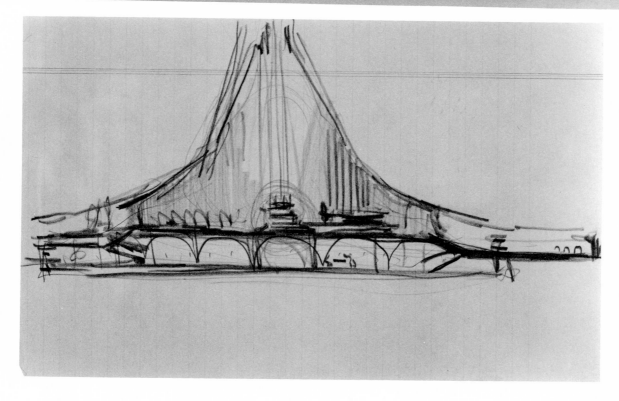

Ａs an airport, the Washington international airport is unique in many ways. It is unique in one way because it is the first commercial airport really to be planned from the start for the jet airplane.

No one asked us to grapple with the problem of a jet-age terminal beyond the question of pure architecture. But I believe the architect has to assume that kind of responsibility. Therefore, together with the team of Ammann & Whitney, engineers, Charles Landrum, airport consultant, and Burns & McDonnell, mechanical engineers, we decided to make a fundamental analysis of the whole problem of a large terminal for jet airplanes. It was a hard-boiled problem and we wanted to solve it in a hard-boiled way.

We sent out teams with counters and stop-watches to see what people really do at airports, how far they walk, their interchange problems. We analyzed special problems of jets, examined schedules, peak loads, effect of weather. We studied baggage handling, economics, methods of operations; and so on. We reduced this vast data to a series of about forty charts.

We found there were three very critical areas. One was the time and inconvenience of getting passengers to and from planes. We discovered the already tremendous distances passengers walk through terminals and the 'fingers' extending from them would become as nothing compared to the distances they would have to walk in jet terminals. Another critical area was the heavy cost of taxiing jet planes. A third consideration was the increasing need for greater possible flexibility in operations and servicing of aircraft.

We became convinced that some new method of passenger handling had to be found. The soundest system seemed to be one which brought the passenger to the plane rather than the plane to the passenger. We discarded the European bus system because it has inconveniences, and we did not want to take a negative step. Gradually, we arrived at the concept of the mobile lounge: a departure lounge on stilts and wheels, a part of the terminal which detaches itself from the building and travels out to wherever the plane is conveniently parked or serviced.

As we investigated further, we became convinced the mobile lounge was a logical solution to the critical problems. We were aware that, like any prototype vehicle, it would be expensive and might have 'bugs.' But we believed it a sound system. We think we have made a real contribution. The mobile lounge can have large application. It can be used in new terminals and it has obvious advantages for the economic, efficient expansion of existing ones.

After the Federal Aviation Agency accepted the idea, we had the formidable job of explaining or 'selling' it to many people within twelve air lines. We worked with Charles Eames, who did a marvelous job, to reduce our data and thinking to a short movie. Clear and exact communication with the client is always important.

This airport is unique in other ways, too. It is unique in being the national and international gateway to the nation's capital. It is unique in its ownership – the Federal Government. It is unique in being a part of the whole complex of buildings that create the image of our nation's capital. We felt the terminal should express all that in its architectural design.

The tradition of Federal architecture is static, but a jet-age airport should be essentially non-static, expressing the movement and the excitement of travel. We thought that if we could bring these two things together into a unified design we would have a very interesting building.

There was also the problem of the site – a beautiful flat plain. In a way, architec-

ture is really placing something between earth and sky. We came to the conclusion that a strong form that seemed both to rise from the plain and to hover over it would look best. The horizontal element, or roof, would be the highest element. It should be tilted forward so the building would be seen. The terminal should also have a monumental scale in this landscape and in the vastness of this huge airfield.

The acceptance of the mobile lounge concept allowed us to make the terminal a single, compact building. We started with abstract ideal shapes for the site and went through many forms – things like a reverse staircase, pyramidal forms – and then many forms that would also work functionally. We wanted a high front covering arriving passengers, because many measly marquees 'rat up' a building. Gradually, we arrived at the idea of a curved roof, high in the front, lower in the middle, slightly higher at the back. It occurred to us that this could be a suspended roof. One had worried that a hanging roof might look heavy from underneath, but the Ingalls Rink, with its sweeping lightness, gave us courage to go to the hanging roof here.

This roof is supported by a row of columns forty feet apart on each side of the concourse, sixty-five feet high on the approach side, forty feet high on the field side. It is like a huge, continuous hammock suspended between concrete trees. It is made of light suspension-bridge cables between which concrete panels of the roof deck fit. The concrete piers are sloped outward to counteract the pull of the cables. But we exaggerated and dramatized this outward slope as well as the wide compressive flange at the rear of the columns to give the colonnade a dynamic and soaring look as well as a stately and dignified one.

But how should this strong, hovering form be placed on the site? How should it be seen from the plain? How should it look as one approached and arrived? The closer you come to some buildings, the less you see. On a functional basis, we had carefully worked out approach ramps on three levels. Esthetically, we realized we could make these ramps into a base for the terminal. Seen from the distance, as one drove down the access road and around the sunken parking lot, the building would seem to rise from this base and assert itself as a hovering form between earth and sky. Approaching closer and arriving, one would see the large colonnade. The control tower (whose form was arrived at after much study) was finally placed at the back of the terminal where it could be seen in changing and good relationships to the terminal from the access and approach roads.

We saw many other problems here as part of the architect's responsibility. There was the problem of the interiors. We felt these should convey the same special and distinctive character we tried to give the architecture itself. Instead of the honky-tonk, Klondike-like chaos of commercial space in most airports, all the interiors and commercial space should be thoughtfully organized to be dignified and attractive. Inside and outside should be all one thing. There was the problem of long-term landscaping, which was worked out with Dan Kiley. There was the crucial problem of disciplined, long-term, and imaginative zoning. Of special importance was the problem of some kind of continuing control in the terminal and its surroundings. We made proposals about these things which I hope will be carried out.

I don't think the terminal should be evaluated just as a work of art. I think we faced this job as an architect's problem in total relation to the present world. We tried to give a completely logical, imaginative, and responsible answer to that problem. I hope as such that we have done a good job. [*Horizon*, July, 1960 and *passim*, July, 1958–March, 1961]

I think this airport is the best thing I have done. I think it is going to be really good. Maybe it will even explain what I believe about architecture. [June 21, 1961]

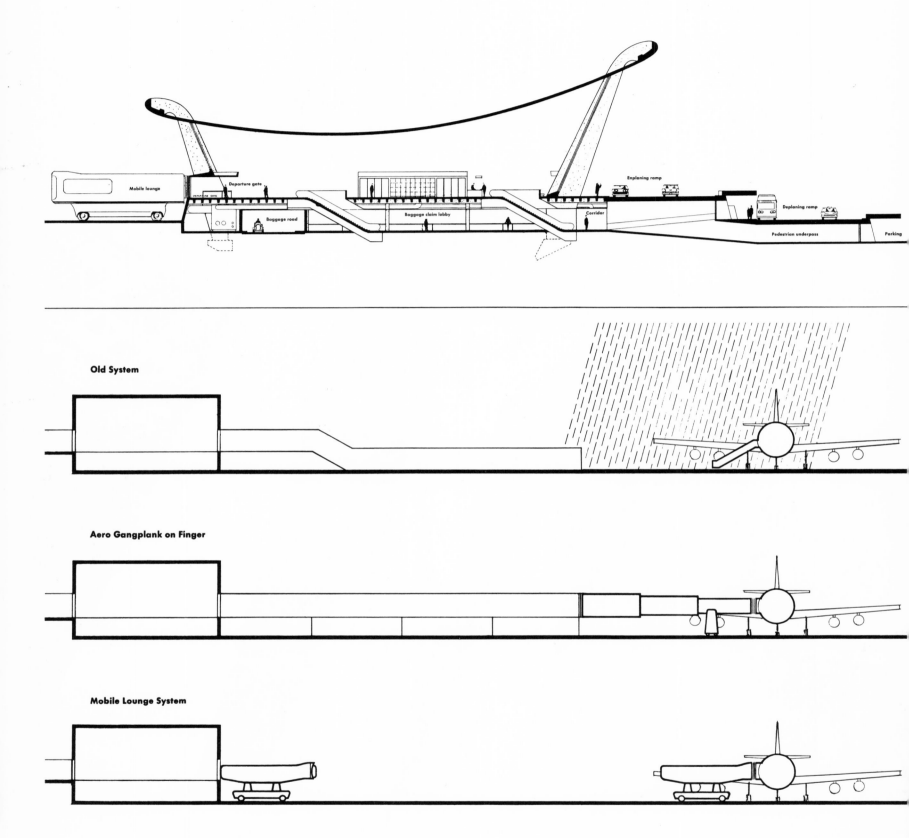

Mobile lounge · Departure gate · Baggage road · Baggage claim lobby · Corridor · Enplaning ramp · Deplaning ramp · Pedestrian underpass · Parking

**Old System**

**Aero Gangplank on Finger**

**Mobile Lounge System**

# Eero Saarinen

A Note
on this Book

Several years ago, on one of our frequent pilgrimages to Frank Lloyd Wright, Mr. Wright told Eero and me why he was wary of interviewers and writers. 'They take the words from your mouth and put them in their own,' he said, 'and, worse than that, they take the smile off your lips and put it on their own.'

When, after Eero's untimely death, various publishers and writers approached me about a book on his work, I remembered Mr. Wright's remarks. Eero, unlike Wright, Le Corbusier, and his own father, had never written books, but it seemed appropriate now to record his own words and smiles and to preserve these forever as his. Such a book would be a document which would allow him to speak as he did so charmingly, so sincerely, so informally to all of us who knew him well; it would illuminate his attitude toward his beloved profession; and it would be a revelation of the creative processes that produced his work. 'We must have an emotional reason as well as a logical end for everything we do,' Eero once said. A book of his own statements could make clear his emotional and his logical intentions. It would not be a definitive history of his work (the time would not be ripe for such a book for at least a decade), but it would be the keystone for all subsequent works.

Such a book, I believed, should be handsomely illustrated with pictures whose primary purpose would be to convey the sense of his intent and the spirit of his buildings.

I was pleased to be able to carry out this project with the Yale University Press, whose sympathy with the idea and whose standards of excellence would surely have gratified Eero.

Aline B. Saarinen
*New Haven, June, 1962*

Biographical
Outline

Born August 20, 1910, at Kirkkonummi, Finland, to Eliel and Loja Gesellius Saarinen.
To United States, 1923; naturalized citizen.
Studied sculpture, Grande Chaumière, Paris, 1930–31.
Bachelor of Fine Arts, Yale University, School of Architecture, 1934.
Charles O. Matcham Fellowship for European travel, 1934–36.
Worked in father's architectural firm, Bloomfield Hills, Michigan, 1936–50.
Principal partner, Eero Saarinen & Associates, 1950–61.
Married Lillian Swann, 1939; children: Eric (1942), Susan (1945); divorced.
Married Aline B. Louchheim, 1953; child: Eames (1954).
Died September 1, 1961, at Ann Arbor, Michigan.

Honors

Master of Arts, Yale University, 1949; Doctor of Humane Letters, Valparaiso University, 1959; Doctor of Humanities, Wayne University, 1961; Doctor of Engineering, Technische Hochschule, Hanover, 1961; Fellow, American Institute of Architects, 1952; Fellow, American Academy of Arts and Letters, 1960; Recipient, Gold Medal of A.I.A., 1962.

Partners

Following Eero Saarinen's death, his partners Joseph N. Lacy and John Dinkeloo, and Chief Designer Kevin Roche, supervised completion of the ten remaining projects.

| | |
|---|---|
| Work in Collaboration with his Father, Eliel Saarinen 1936–1950 | First Christian Church, Columbus, Indiana, 1939 |
| | Crow Island School, Winnetka, Illinois, 1939 |
| | Antioch College, Yellow Springs, Ohio; Campus Plan, 1946; Dormitory, 1947 |
| | Brandeis University, Waltham, Massachusetts; Campus Plan, 1948; Dormitory, Dining and Social Buildings, 1949–50 |
| | Berkshire Music Center, Lenox, Massachusetts; Opera Shed, 1940 |
| | Christ Church Lutheran, Minneapolis, Minnesota, 1949 |
| | Smithsonian Art Gallery, Washington, D.C. (First Prizewinning Design), 1939 |

**Independent Work 1941–1964**

Project, Community House, 1941

Project, Unfolding House, 1945

Music Tent, Aspen, Colorado, 1949 (*Page 7*)

Jefferson National Expansion Memorial, St. Louis, Missouri, 1948–1964 (*Pages 18–23*)

General Motors Technical Center, Warren, Michigan, 1948–1956 (Smith, Hinchman & Grylls, Architect-Engineers) (*Pages 24–33*)

Drake University, Des Moines, Iowa; Pharmacy Building, 1947–1950; Dormitories and Dining Hall, 1951–1955

Irwin Union Trust Company, Columbus, Indiana, 1952–1955

Massachusetts Institute of Technology, Cambridge, Massachusetts; Auditorium and Chapel, 1953–1956 (*Pages 34–39*)

Master Plan, University of Michigan, Ann Arbor, Michigan, 1954

Milwaukee County War Memorial, Milwaukee, Wisconsin, 1953–1957 (*Pages 40–43*)

Stephens College Chapel, Columbia, Missouri, 1953–1957

Residence in Midwest, 1953–1957

Concordia Senior College, Fort Wayne, Indiana, 1953–1958 (*Pages 44–47*)

Vassar College, Poughkeepsie, New York; Dormitory, 1954–58

University of Chicago, Illinois; Women's Dormitory and Dining Hall, 1955–58

U.S. Chancellery Building, Oslo, Norway, 1955–59 (*Pages 52 and 53*)

U.S. Chancellery Building, London, England, 1955–60 (*Pages 48–51*)

University of Chicago, Illinois; Law School, 1956–60

International Business Machines, Rochester, Minnesota, 1956–59

David S. Ingalls Hockey Rink, Yale University, New Haven, Connecticut, 1956–59 (*Pages 54–59*)

Trans World Flight Center, Idlewild, New York, 1956–62 (*Pages 60–67*)

University of Pennsylvania, Philadelphia, Pennsylvania; Women's Dormitories, 1957–60

Deere & Company, Moline, Illinois, 1957–63 (*Pages 76–79*)

Thomas J. Watson Research Center, International Business Machines, Yorktown, New York, 1957–61 (*Pages 70–75*)

Bell Laboratories, Holmdel, New Jersey, 1957–62

Ezra Stiles and Morse Colleges, Yale University, New Haven, Connecticut, 1958–62 (*Pages 80–87*)

Dulles International Airport Terminal Building, Chantilly, Virginia, 1958–62 (Ammann & Whitney, Architect-Engineers) (*Pages 92–103*)

Repertory Theatre and Library Museum, Lincoln Center for the Performing Arts, New York City, 1958–64 (Skidmore, Owings & Merrill, Associated Architects; Jo Mielziner, Collaborating Designer for Repertory Theatre)

International Airport, Athens, Greece, 1960–64 (Ammann & Whitney, Architect-Engineers)

North Christian Church, Columbus, Indiana, 1959–63 (*Pages 88–91*)

Columbia Broadcasting System, Headquarters Building, New York City, 1960–64 (*Pages 16 and 17*)

**Furniture Design**

Organic Design Furniture, Museum of Modern Art Competition, with Charles Eames, 1938

For Knoll Associates: Plywood Chair, 1946; "Womb" Chair, 1948; Pedestal Furniture, 1958 (*Page 68*)

Chairs for G.M.T.C. Lobbies, 1950

*Designed by Alvin Eisenman*